Profitable Passive Income

Strategies for Financial Success

Table of Contents

Chapter 1. Introduction

Welcome to your gateway to becoming financially independent! Our Special Report: "Profitable Passive Income: Strategies for Financial Success" is a comprehensive guide designed to set you on the pathway to lasting prosperity. The exciting part is, we've compiled a variety of simplified, yet effective strategies - no technical jargon here! This report is all about letting your money work for you while you sit back and enjoy the fruits of smart investing. Written in a straightforward, engaging style, it promises to positively revolutionize the way you view and manage your finances. Get ready to transform your financial future by unlocking the secrets of generating sustainable, long-term passive income. This is the investment you need today for a worry-free tomorrow! Endorse yourself, purchase this report, and embark on a journey paved with possibilities, potential, and financial success!

Chapter 2. Understanding Passive Income: A Comprehensive Overview

Understanding the cornerstone of financial independence begins with grasping what passive income is. For many, the term might seem elusive or highly technical, invoking images of Wall Street and convoluted financial instruments. Abstaining from the technical vernacular, at its core, passive income is income generated from minimal to no effort from the recipient after an initial investment of time, money, or both. Think of it as hiring your money to work for you around the clock. Still sounds complex? Let's break it down into simplified concepts - the types of income, what constitutes passive income, and the benefits it offers.

2.1. Types of Income

In the pursuit of comprehending passive income, it's crucial to distinguish it from its two counterparts - active and portfolio income.

Active income, most people's source of sustenance, is money earned from providing a service, like wages, tips, salaries, or profits from businesses where there is material participation from the owner.

Then comes portfolio income received from investments, dividends, interest, and capital gains from selling securities at a profit. While it may seem passive, the classification remains different because it often requires significant input and management.

2.2. What Constitutes Passive Income

Passive income, the star player of this report, is earnings derived from a rental property, limited partnership, or other enterprises in which the person is not actively involved. Creating an eBook, developing a mobile application, renting out property, or investing in a high-yielding fixed deposit are some diverse examples of passive income sources.

Essentially, passive income sources are like well-oiled machines for wealth generation; after an initial investment of time and resources, they require minimal effort to maintain. This takes us to the next crucial question – why passive income?

2.3. Benefits of Passive Income

To cement passive income's importance, we delve into its benefits.

1. **Financial Security**: Passive income diversifies your income streams. This means even if one source experiences a downturn, others can compensate, providing a safety net.

2. **Freedom of Time**: Unlike a 9-to-5 job, passive income doesn't demand continuous effort. This encourages better work-life balance, creating time for family, hobbies, and personal development.

3. **Early Retirement**: With sufficient passive income, conventional retirement ages no longer dictate your life's trajectory.

4. **Risk Mitigation**: An arsenal of passive income sources can help weather financial crises, market volatility, and unexpected job losses.

2.4. Creating Passive Income

To begin your passive income journey, understanding the 'how' is just as important as the 'what' and 'why'. It involves a simple, yet dynamic, process:

1. **Finding a Suitable Source**: Researching to identify the perfect passive income source that aligns with your interests, skills, and financial goals.

2. **Making the Initial Investment**: Putting in the necessary time, money, or both, to set up your passive income source.

3. **Management and Monitoring**: Ensuring the source runs smoothly. This might involve occasional check-ups or necessary adjustments.

2.5. Different Passive Income Models

While the range of passive income sources is varied and extensive, most fall under one of these categories:

1. **Investment Income**: These include assets that appreciate in value over time or provide a regular return, such as bonds, index funds, dividend-yielding stocks, and rental properties.

2. **Business Income**: This includes startup businesses, online stores, or rental properties that generate consistent revenue after initial setup and minimal maintenance.

3. **Royalty Income**: This category is for musicians, authors, and inventors who get a commission every time their work is used.

2.6. Final Thoughts

Remember, this journey to financial independence isn't instant. It requires patience, persistence, and unreserved commitment. However, once set up, these streams of passive income will feed into your wealth, transforming not just your finances but your life.

Where many see barriers, you'll see stepping stones. And that shift—going from living paycheck to paycheck to approaching every monetary choice with strategic insight—is the transformation that understanding passive income allows. Financial success, freedom, and security await on the other side of action. In the following chapters, we will delve deeper into each passive income model, helping you find and form the ones perfect for you. Welcome to a future designed by you, for you!

Note: This guide aims to educate and inspire you on your financial journey. It is, however, not a substitute for professional advice catered to your unique financial situation.

Chapter 3. Life-changing Financial Concepts: Introduction to Passive Investing

Passive investing, by definition, is a long-term investment strategy in which an investor buys a portfolio of securities and holds onto them for a significant period of time, regardless of market fluctuations. Often referred to as a "buy and hold" strategy, it's the polar opposite of active investing. Active investing involves trying to beat the market by buying and selling securities based on market predictions, changes in the economy, or events that could impact the stock's price. The goal of passive investing is to generate income over the long term by keeping the amount of buying and selling to a minimum.

3.1. Why Choose Passive Investing?

The attraction of passive investing lies in its simplicity and cost-effectiveness. You're not spending time, energy, and potentially a lot of money trying to pick the next big winner or dodge the market's dips and swings. Instead, you're adopting a long-term approach, which means lower transaction costs and less time spent managing investments.

One of the keys behind this strategy is the belief in market efficiency - that the current market price of a security accurately reflects all the information available about it and that any changes to this information are reflected in the price immediately. If you subscribe to this theory, then attempting to "beat the market" becomes pointless as the market, in theory, can't be outperformed consistently over the long term.

Another aspect to consider is the cost-effectiveness. Active investing often involves short-term trading, which can lead to significant costs, including brokerage fees and capital gains taxes. On the other hand, passive investing typically incurs lower costs because you're holding onto investments longer. This means fewer transaction fees and a lower tax bill.

3.2. How Does Passive Investing Work?

There's no one-size-fits-all strategy when it comes to passive investing – it mainly depends on individual financial goals, risk tolerance, and time horizon. However, there are certain common steps involved in constructing a passive investment portfolio.

The first step is to determine an appropriate asset allocation, i.e., the mix of various types of investments you'll have in your portfolio. The most common form of asset allocation involves a mix of stocks and bonds. The proportion depends on factors such as your age, risk tolerance, and how many years you have until retirement.

Once you've determined your asset allocation, the second step is to diversify your investments. Diversification helps reduce risk. For instance, if you invest all your savings in one type of stock, and that stock goes down in value, your entire portfolio would be affected. But if your portfolio includes a wide variety of investments, a decline in one would be balanced out by gains in another.

Investing in exchange-traded funds (ETFs) or index funds is one of the most common strategies for diversification. These funds are designed to track the performance of a specific index, such as the S&P 500. Because they offer exposure to a broad range of stocks, they provide instant diversification.

The third step in passive investing is periodic rebalancing to ensure your portfolio remains aligned with your chosen asset allocation. For example, if your desired allocation is 70 percent stocks and 30 percent bonds, and the stock portion grows to 75 percent as a result of a bull market, you would sell some stocks and buy bonds to readjust your portfolio back to the 70:30 ratio.

3.3. The Simple Power of Compound Interest

One of the most critical financial concepts to understand when considering passive investing is compound interest. Often referred to as the "eighth wonder of the world", it plays an integral part in passive investing and long-term financial growth. Compound interest enables you to earn interest on both the original amount of money you invested and the interest you continue to earn.

Consider this example: if you invest $10,000 at an interest rate of 7% annually, you would earn $700 in the first year. If you leave that money invested, in the second year, you would earn interest not just on your initial $10,000, but also on the $700 of interest from the first year. So, your second year's interest would be $749 ($10,700 x 7%), bringing your total investment to $11,449 after two years.

The power of compound interest amplifies over time, benefiting those who invest early and stay invested. It reiterates the importance of patience in the investing universe and how passively 'sitting' on your investments can help your wealth multiply exponentially over long periods.

3.4. Risks and Limits to Passive Investing

Like any investment strategy, passive investing carries its share of risks and limitations. One of the most significant risks of passive investment is market risk. As a passive investor, you are exposed to the trends of the market. When the market falls, so will your investment.

Another limitation pertains to earning potential. While passive investing generally earns a stable return, it may not be capable of delivering massive short-term profits like active investing can in a bull market.

However, one must remember that turmoil in financial markets is often temporary, while the trajectory of increase is usually upward in the long term. As famed investor Warren Buffet rightly puts it, "Our favorite holding period is forever." Passivity can indeed be a virtue when it comes to investment, as proven by the success stories of countless men and women who have built enduring wealth, not by attempting to time the market, but by giving their investments time to grow and bear fruit.

Now that we've covered the basics of passive investing, it's important to remember that education is an ongoing journey. Remain curious, remain studious. Remember, passive investing isn't passive learning. The more you know about financial markets and investing strategies, the better equipped you will be to build a portfolio that meets your needs and helps you achieve your financial goals.

Chapter 4. Creating Passive Income through Real Estate Investments

Real estate investment can be a mighty tool in your quest for financial independence through passive income. The key to unlocking its potential lies in understanding the nuts and bolts of the industry. For this, one needs to delve into the depths of various strategies, risks, rewards, and more.

4.1. Understanding Real Estate Investment

Investing in real estate primarily involves purchasing a property and then earning income by leasing or selling it. This kind of investment has been a cornerstone of wealth creation for centuries, largely thanks to its ability to provide consistent cash flow, the potential for price appreciation over time, and beneficial tax advantages.

Before laying the first brick of your real estate empire, it's essential to understand that this type of investment does require a significant upfront cost. But once the initial investment is made, properties can provide regular, largely passive income in the form of rent payments from tenants.

4.2. Types of Real Estate Investments

Now that we've grasped the basic gist of real estate investment, let's navigate through its various types. The type of real estate investment strategy you select will largely depend on your financial goals, your tolerance for risk, and your investment acumen.

- Residential Real Estate: This involves investing in properties such as houses, apartments, townhouses, and vacation homes where a resident pays rent for living. Generally, the rental agreements are set for a year, offering a relatively stable source of income.

- Commercial Real Estate: These are properties used solely for business purposes. This could cover anything from a single store to a huge shopping mall. The leases for commercial properties are typically longer than residential ones, ensuring more steady and reliable income.

- Industrial Real Estate: This includes everything from industrial warehouses to large-scale industrial compounds and buildings. Although these investments might have higher maintenance costs, the potential for income can be substantial given the scale of operations that these properties cater to.

- Raw Land Investments: This involves buying land and creating value in a variety of ways, such as developing housing or a commercial property, subdividing and selling parcels, or simply holding onto it with the hope of selling it later at a higher price. However, it comes with a significant amount of risk and may require a lofty initial investment.

4.3. Strategies in Real Estate Investment

Once you've identified the type of real estate investment that suits your financial objectives, it's time to delve into strategies. Successful real estate investing involves more than just purchasing properties – it requires a strategic approach.

4.3.1. Investment Strategy 1: Rental Properties

This is arguably the most direct method of generating passive income through real estate. Here, you buy a property and rent it out to a tenant. Generally speaking, the landlord, i.e., the property owner, is responsible for paying the mortgage, taxes, and costs of maintaining the property.

4.3.2. Investment Strategy 2: Real Estate Investment Trusts (REITs)

If you're interested in real estate investment but want to avoid the responsibilities that come with owning a property, investing in a REIT may be a good option. In essence, REITs are companies that own and manage a portfolio of real estate properties and mortgages. Shares in REITs are bought and sold on the major exchanges, just like a stock. As a shareholder, you can earn a share of the income produced without actually having to buy or manage a property yourself.

4.3.3. Investment Strategy 3: Flipping Houses

This strategy involves buying properties at a relatively low price, most likely because they require some repair or maintenance, and then quickly reselling them at a profit. It's a hands-on approach and may require a strong understanding of real estate markets to be successful. The key is to purchase a home below market value, ensure that the cost of repairs does not supersede your profit margin, and sell at a high price.

4.4. How to Start Your Real Estate Investment Journey

Now we come to a pivotal question – how does one get started with real estate investment? It requires a thoughtful step-by-step approach that includes research, planning, and, finally, execution.

4.4.1. Step 1: Financial Planning

Before you even start looking at properties, it's essential to understand your financial situation. A comprehensive review of your financial health will help you determine how much you can afford to invest. Make sure to include savings, income, expenses, and any outstanding debts in your review.

4.4.2. Step 2: Detailed Research

Understanding real estate markets can be complex. Begin your process with detailed research about the type of property you're interested in, potential locations, market trends, property value estimations, and rental yield.

4.4.3. Step 3: Assemble a reliable team

Even if you're planning on managing properties by yourself, it's always helpful to have a team of professionals. It may include a real estate attorney, an accountant, property inspectors, and real estate agents.

4.4.4. Step 4: Secure Financing

Depending upon your financial plan, you may need to secure financing for your investment. Your options might include traditional mortgages, investor-friendly loans, or even personal loans. Always shop around for the best rates before finalizing a loan.

4.4.5. Step 5: Purchase the Property

Once all the previous steps are meticulously followed, you can go ahead and close the deal on your selected property.

Investing in the real estate sector can be an excellent way to achieve financial independence if approached with diligence, patience, knowledge, and strategic planning. However, like all investment channels, it comes with risks. The golden rule is to keep educating yourself, diversify your investment opportunities, and keep a clear vision of your financial objectives.

Chapter 5. Stocks, Bonds and Dividends: A Guide to Financial Instruments

In the world of financial management and wealth creation, three of the most integral instruments are stocks, bonds, and dividends. These pivotal pillars – while they may seem baffling initially – offer exceptional opportunities for generating passive income and building wealth. To navigate this fascinating yet complex arena, it is crucial to understand what these financial instruments are, their working mechanisms, the differences among them, and the ways to leverage them effectively for maximum gain.

5.1. Understanding Stocks

'Buying a piece of a company,' this simple phrase elegantly captures what acquiring stocks or shares implies. As a stockholder, you're effectively a partial owner of a firm and have a stake in its success. However, with stakes come risks—the fortunes of your investment largely hinge on the company's financial health.

There are two primary types of stocks: common and preferred. Whereas common stockholders often have voting rights in the company, preferred stockholders don't. On the dividend side, preferred stockholders usually receive them at a fixed rate before any distribution is made to common stockholders.

5.2. The Dynamics of Bonds

In essence, a bond is a loan you provide to an entity, generally a government or a corporation. In return for the borrowed money, you are promised regular interest payments, usually semi-annually, until the loan's maturity date. At maturity, the principal amount is returned.

Now, the attractiveness of bonds as an investment avenue lies primarily in their relative safety compared to stocks. While stocks can give unprecedented returns, they can also plummet sharply. Bonds, on the other hand, provide steadiness and reliability with regular interest income and a guaranteed return of the principal upon maturity.

5.3. Impact of Dividends

A slice of a company's profits shared with its stockholders is known as a dividend. Ordinarily paid in cash, dividends represent the company's commitment to its stakeholders and are powerful lures for potential investors.

Two key metrics concerning dividends are essential for an investor—the dividend yield and the payout ratio. The dividend yield relates annual dividends to the stock's present price, allowing investors to compare returns across different stocks based on dividends. The payout ratio, comparing the annual dividends to the company's earnings, indicates the sustainability of these dividends.

5.4. The Interplay: Stocks, Bonds, and Dividends

Now, each of these financial instruments has a distinct role in one's investment portfolio and can harmoniously fulfill different requirements.

Stocks are wealth generators — given the right choice, ample time, and market conditions, they can magnify an initial investment manifolds. However, they also carry substantial risks, making them suited for those willing to embrace volatility for higher returns.

Bonds are wealth preservers — while they lack the explosive growth potential of stocks, they provide stability and predictable returns. Bonds work exceptionally well for conservative investors seeking gradual wealth accumulation without major risks.

Dividends serve as supplementary income — consistent dividends from well-established companies can serve as a steady passive income source, bolstering the total returns from stock investments.

In creating a well-diversified portfolio, a balanced mix of stocks, bonds, and dividend-paying shares can augment the growth potential while mitigating risks. The appropriate composition depends on your financial goals, risk tolerance, and investment horizon.

5.5. Strategies for Stock Picking

While stock picking can often appear as a gamble to the untrained eye, a strategic, rule-based approach can significantly improve your odds. At the base level, this involves analyzing the stock's value, financial performance, industry position, and future growth prospects.

Fundamental analysis and technical analysis are two widely used methods for stock selection. While fundamental analysis focuses on a company's financial health and economic indicators, technical analysis involves studying price trends and patterns to predict future price movements.

5.6. Bond Investment Tactics

A successful bond investment strategy considers the bond's yield, its issuer's creditworthiness, term, and price. Furthermore, recognizing the interplay between interest rates and bond prices is crucial. Generally, bond prices and interest rates move in opposite directions.

Bonds can be part of an income strategy where the investor seeks regular interest payments or a defensive strategy to safeguard against potential market volatility. Also, a relatively lesser known strategy is bond laddering, where investments are spaced across bonds with different maturity dates.

5.7. Harnessing Dividends for Passive Income

Blue-chip companies, renowned for their market leadership, stable financial health, and propensity to pay regular, substantial dividends, can be excellent sources for passive income. Nonetheless, the investors must avoid 'dividend traps'—high dividend yield may be due to a plunging stock price, which indicates problems.

Moreover, take advantage of DRIPs (Dividend Reinvestment Plans). By automatically reinvesting dividends in more shares, DRIPs harness the magic of compounding and sequentially boost your investment's growth.

Venturing into stocks, bonds, and dividends is akin to embarking on a thrilling voyage with enormous rewards waiting along the way. It requires understanding, strategy, and, above all, time to let compounding weave its magic. Nevertheless, the journey is immensely fulfilling and can pave the way to financial independence, shaping the life you envision.

Chapter 6. P2P Lending and Crowdfunding: Modern Passive Income Streams

P2P (Peer-to-Peer) lending and crowdfunding have emerged as modern avenues for generating passive income. Here, technology plays a fascinating role in connecting people who have funds to invest with those who need them. This direct connection has opened up new possibilities for investors looking for unique, profitable streams of passive income.

6.1. The Rise of P2P Lending

P2P lending, also known as crowdlending, is a method of lending where individuals directly lend to other individuals or businesses via an online platform, without the need for a traditional financial institution as an intermediary.

The success of P2P lending is largely due to the higher rate of returns it offers to investors compared to traditional investment options. As an investor, you could earn annual yields of 5% to 8% or even more. This rate is extremely competitive when put up against returns from other traditional forms of investments like bonds or savings accounts.

Lending platforms facilitate this process by conducting risk assessments, dividing loans into affordable chunks and collecting repayments. They charge service fees to earn their keep. Top P2P platforms include Prosper, LendingClub and Funding Circle.

6.2. How P2P Lending Works

Investors begin by signing up on a P2P lending platform. They then browse potential loan recipients, reading the platform's assessment of each loan's risk category and potential interest. Once they've selected recipients they'd like to lend to, investors allocate funds to these loans. Then, they sit back and let the platform gather the repayments for them.

There are typically two types of P2P lending: . Secured lending: The loans are tied to assets, which could be seized in case of default. . Unsecured lending: The loans are not tied to any assets.

By diversifying your investments across various loanees and sectors, you can mitigate the risk of defaults.

6.3. The Appeal of Crowdfunding

While P2P lending is a type of debt crowdfunding, other forms of crowdfunding exist that present opportunities for passive income. The three most common are equity, donation, and reward crowdfunding.

1. Equity crowdfunding: Investors become shareholders in the company they invest in, acquiring a portion of its equity. They stand to profit if the company eventually sells out or goes public.

2. Donation crowdfunding: Persons fund causes they care about, without expectations for financial returns.

3. Reward crowdfunding: Backers pledge money to a creative project or product in development and receive rewards in return.

For passive income seekers, equity crowdfunding stands out. Here, investors become part owners of startups or small businesses they finance, enjoying dividends or capital gains when these businesses become successful.

Like all investment vehicles, P2P lending and crowdfunding have their pros and risks.

The upsides are potential high returns, access to novel investment opportunities, and the ability to start with small sums. The diversification opportunities are another clear advantage.

Risks include borrower defaults in P2P lending and business failures in crowdfunding. The relatively low transparency and regulation may also be concerns.

The key to success in this arena lies in diversification. Don't put all your eggs in one basket — spread your investments across a wide array of borrowers or businesses.

Passive income seekers who emphasize on high returns and who are willing to take on some calculated risk may find P2P lending and crowdfunding attractive. Although they come with their fair share of risks, adequate due diligence and a diversified approach can drastically improve the potential for solid returns.

6.4. Conclusion

In summation, P2P lending and crowdfunding represent exciting opportunities for the modern investor. By understanding these channels and navigating them wisely, you can tap into these cutting-edge streams of passive income. With the right strategy and a risk-managed approach, they can prove to be promising avenues for financial growth and prosperity.

Invest wisely, begin with small sums and always diversify. In time, you may find that this modern form of investing not only provides a nice supplement to your income but also introduces you to exciting sectors and innovative businesses. Although P2P lending and crowdfunding are not devoid of risks, they certainly have their fair share of potentials only waiting to be uncapped by astute investors.

Always remember, the key to financial freedom lies not just in working hard for money, but also having your money working hard for you. And that, dear reader, is the true essence of passive income generation.

Chapter 7. Becoming an Affiliate Marketer: Monetizing Your Online Presence

Generating passive income from affiliate marketing involves leveraging your online presence to promote products or services offered by other companies. When a visitor engages with the affiliated links you share (by clicking on the link, signing up for a product, making a purchase, etc.) and completes an agreed-upon action, you earn a commission. An essential aspect of affiliate marketing is selecting the right products or services to endorse - ones that align with your platform content and are likely to appeal to your target audience.

7.1. The Basics of Affiliate Marketing

First and foremost, let's clarify what affiliate marketing is and how it makes money. In essence, you, as an affiliate, establish a partnership with a company looking to sell its products or services. This partnership allows you to earn a commission for every sale that occurs through your referral.

How do you get these referrals and sales? That's where your online presence comes in. Be it a blog, a YouTube channel, a podcast, or a social media platform; you share the company's products or services with your audience, using a unique affiliate link provided by the company. When a visitor successfully completes a purchase through this link, you make money.

7.2. Choosing the Right Affiliate Marketing Program

The affiliate marketing landscape is vast, and finding the right affiliate program is crucial for success. There are several types of affiliate programs, each with its pros and cons. These include:

- Cost per Click (CPC): Here, you earn whenever a visitor clicks on your affiliate link, regardless of whether they make a purchase.

- Cost per Action (CPA): In this model, you earn a commission when a visitor completes a specific action, like signing up for a service or subscribing to a newsletter.

- Cost per Sale (CPS): As the name implies, you earn when a visitor completes a purchase through your affiliate link.

Be sure to research extensively and select programs that suit not only your interests but also the interests of your audience. Aligning your chosen product or service with your platform is a key factor in determining your success as an affiliate marketer.

7.3. Building Your Online Presence

Before diving headlong into affiliate marketing, it's important to have a solid foundation to build on. This foundation is your online presence. Start by determining where you'll promote affiliate products or services. Are you an active blogger, or do you have a thriving YouTube channel? Do you have a sizeable Instagram following, or are you the owner of a popular website?

Once you've established the platform(s) where you'll promote your chosen affiliate products, it's time to grow your online presence. This growth comes mainly from consistently sharing valuable content that resonates with your audience and gradually builds their trust. Remember, the goal isn't to push sales but to form relationships with your audience and provide value.

7.4. Becoming An Influencer: Building Trust and Credibility

In a world filled with marketing messages, consumers are increasingly turning to individuals they respect - influencers - to cut through the noise. As an affiliate marketer, you can effectively tap into this growing trend by becoming a trusted influencer in your niche.

Becoming an influencer isn't about having thousands or millions of followers. Rather, it's about having a meaningful engagement with your followers. Offering valuable content and feedback will earn you their trust, and once you have this trust, you'll be well-positioned to generate passive income as an affiliate marketer.

To become a credible influencer in your niche, consistently share high-quality content related to your chosen niche, engage with your followers in meaningful ways, actively participate in conversations, and support your audience when possible.

7.5. Affiliate Marketing Best Practices: Dos and Don'ts

Being successful in affiliate marketing isn't just about following a set routine; it's about implementing best practices that maximize your chances of success while avoiding common pitfalls. Here are a few:

Do's: - Select relevant products or services: Choose products that are relevant to your niche and your audience's interests. - Be truthful and transparent: Always be open about your affiliations. Honesty not only builds trust with your audience but also complies with disclosure requirements by the FTC. - Give honest reviews: Affiliate marketing is not about blindly promoting a product or service. Share your genuine experiences and opinions about the products or services you promote.

Don'ts: - Don't over-promote: Bombarding your audience with sales pitches will likely drive them away. Balance your content with valuable information and product promotions. - Don't expect immediate success: Affiliate marketing is typically a long game. Be patient and persistent.

To summarize, becoming an affiliate marketer requires a solid foundation of an existing online presence, choosing the right affiliate marketing program, and creating a platform of trust with your audience. It may take time and require patience, effort, and dedication. But with the right approach, your affiliate marketing venture could become your main source of passive income, setting you on the road to financial freedom.

Chapter 8. Maximizing Passive Income through Rental Properties

Investing in rental properties can be a powerful strategy to generate passive income and achieve financial independence. However, to truly maximize your income and profits, you need to approach this method intelligently and strategically. Let's delve deep into the various aspects of rental property investment, from selecting the right properties to handling regulations, taxes, and potential risk factors.

8.1. Finding the Perfect Rental Property

When it comes to rental properties, finding the right property is crucial. Location is the key determinant of a property's potential for generating a steady stream of passive income. A property located in a growing neighborhood or city with a strong job market can command higher rents. It's important to research demographic trends, economic indicators, and real estate market trends for any location you're considering.

Proximity to amenities like schools, parks, shopping, and other attractions can also increase a property's desirability for potential renters. Property type is another crucial factor. Single-family homes, multi-family homes, condos, and commercial properties each have their unique advantages and drawbacks in terms of rental income, maintenance costs, and market demand.

8.2. Financing Your Rental Property Investment

Rental property investing can demand significant upfront capital investment. Therefore, understanding your financing options is vital. Traditional mortgages, hard money loans, private money loans, and real estate investment crowdfunding platforms are various financing methods available.

Before deciding on a financing method, consider factors such as interest rate, loan term, monthly payment, and the impact on your cash flow. Remember, the ultimate goal is to ensure a positive cash flow, income that exceeds your property-related expenses.

8.3. Critical Calculations to Consider

Understanding a handful of real estate investing metrics can dramatically impact your ability to maximize passive income. Here are a few critical calculations:

- Cash Flow: The amount of money that remains after deducting all expenses associated with the property from the rental income.

- Cash-on-Cash Return (CoC): This measures the annual return you made on your property in relation to the down-payment invested.

- Capitalization Rate (Cap Rate): This is the ratio between the income a property generates (net of operating expenses) and its purchase price. A higher Cap Rate often implies a better investment.

- Return on Investment (ROI): This shows the percentage of invested money that's returned to an investor. ROI integrates the concept of total return into decision-making.

8.4. Effective Property Management

Effective property management can reduce hassle, minimize vacancies, and boost your rental income. Property management duties can be time-consuming, but they can be outsourced to professional property management firms.

These companies handle tenant selection, rent collection, property maintenance, and dealing with legal issues, making your investment truly passive. However, property management services come at a cost, usually a percentage of the monthly rental income. It's essential to factor these costs into your expense calculations.

8.5. Tax Implications and Advantages

Various expenses incurred in managing a rental income property, such as mortgage interest, property taxes, insurance, maintenance expenses, property management fees, and depreciation, can be tax-deductible. These tax deductions can help offset rental income, reducing your overall tax liability.

However, there are rules and implications to consider, such as depreciation recapture when you sell the property and "passive activity" rules that limit how much you can offset other income. Consult a tax professional to ensure you fully understand the tax implications and can optimize your tax advantages.

8.6. Keeping Vacancies to a Minimum

Maintaining low vacancy rates is crucial for maximizing passive rental income. Prolonged vacancies can strain your cash flow and even lead to losses. Practices such as competitive pricing, proactive marketing, and tenant retention strategies can help you avoid vacancies or at least minimize their duration.

8.7. Dealing with Repairs and Maintenance

Effective maintenance and prompt repairs are not only crucial for preserving the value of your property but also for staying competitive in the rental market. Tenants are more likely to renew leases for properties that are well-maintained. Proactive maintenance also reduces the frequency and cost of repairs over time.

8.8. Conclusion

Investing in rental properties can be a profitable venture, promising a steady stream of passive income. However, success requires more than just owning a property and charging rent. It demands strategic property selection, efficient management, smart financing decisions, prudent risk management, and skilled tax planning.

Yes, there's plenty to learn and explore. Yet, with each step taken, with every move made, and through every hurdle surpassed, you'll find yourself on a path adorned with the rewards of patience, discipline, and strategic exploits - the rewards of sustained, substantial, and mind-growing passive income. So dive deep, dive smart, and watch money, in its most profitable form, flow incessantly into the reservoir of your wealth.

Chapter 9. Delving into Dividend Stocks: A Beginner's Guide

Understanding the concept of dividend stocks is the first step in your journey towards financial independence through passive income. As the name implies, these are stocks from companies that offer dividends - payments made out of earnings and distributed among shareholders. This type of investment enables you to earn while you own, regardless of the stock's movements in price.

9.1. The Basics of Dividend Stocks

A dividend is a portion of a company's earnings that is distributed to shareholders, typically in the form of cash or additional shares. Not every company pays out dividends. Those that do are often well-established and financially stable, fostering investor trust.

Dividend stocks are a fantastic way to generate passive income. Once you purchase these stocks, you can look forward to a steady stream of income through dividend payouts. That's in addition to any potential capital gains if the stock's price increases.

Dividend yields (the dividend payment per share divided by the stock's price per share) are a critical metric when investing in dividend-paying stocks. High dividend yield can indicate a good return on investment. Still, investors need to ensure the company's dividends are sustainable since an extraordinarily high yield may be a red flag that the company is experiencing financial difficulties.

9.2. Choosing the Right Dividend Stocks

Deciding which dividend stocks to invest in is no simple task. Accumulating information about the company, understanding its financial metrics, and monitoring its performance are all integral steps in this process. Below are some important factors to consider:

Dividend Yield: Measure the potential return on your investment. However, be wary of stocks with exceptionally high yields as they may not be sustainable.

Dividend Growth: Companies that have a history of consistently increasing dividend payments year after year can provide more reliable income and are likely in a healthy financial position.

Payout Ratio: This is the percentage of the company's earnings that are paid out as dividends. A payout ratio under 100% suggests the company has ample funds to sustain and potentially increase dividends.

Earnings Growth: Companies with steady earnings growth will likely continue paying dividends.

Company Stability: Well-established companies with a history of stable cash flow are more likely to pay consistent dividends.

9.3. Building a Dividend Portfolio

Constructing a balanced and diversified dividend portfolio is foundational for long-term financial success. Here's how to achieve that:

Start Small and Diversify: Start by investing a small amount in different companies across various sectors. This reduces risk through diversification.

Consider Dividend Growth: Investing in companies that consistently increase their dividends can lead to a growing income stream over time.

Reinvest Dividends: Consider using dividend payouts to purchase more shares. This is known as a Dividend Reinvestment Plan (DRIP), and it compounds your returns over time.

Balancing Yield and Growth: Purchase a mix of high-yield and high-growth stocks to strike a balance between income generation and capital appreciation.

Monitor Your Investments: Keep an eye on the company's financial situation and be ready to adjust your holdings when necessary.

9.4. Dividends and Taxes

Since dividends are income, they are subject to taxes. There are two types of dividends for tax purposes: qualified and non-qualified. Qualified dividends are taxed at a lower rate because they come from stocks you've held for over 60 days, while non-qualified dividends are taxed as regular income. Understanding the tax implications of your investments can help you maximize your returns.

Unraveling the world of dividend stocks uncovers many opportunities for profitable passive income. Building and balancing a robust dividend stock portfolio can help you achieve your financial goals and create a sustainable income stream. Educating yourself is the first step to success in this field, and with patience and persistence, you'll be able to navigate the market confidently. Remember, investments in dividend stocks are not a race to riches, but a steady path towards long-term financial independence.

Chapter 10. Building a Profitable Blog: A Road to Passive Earnings

Blogging has evolved from a hobbyist venture into a legitimate business model. More than just a platform to express ideas or interests, blogs have the potential to generate substantial revenue, creating a viable stream of passive income for their owners. Here, we delve into how you can create and monetize your own blog to pave the way towards financial independence.

10.1. Initial Setup

Before you start your blog, you need to make some key decisions. Choose a niche that you're passionate about and that has commercial value. Next, pick a catchy and memorable name for your blog. Once you settle on a name, check if the domain name is available and buy it.

In terms of selecting a blogging platform, WordPress is highly recommended due to its customization capabilities and vast collection of themes and plugins. Furthermore, you'll need web hosting. A "managed" WordPress hosting platform might be worth considering as it comes with better security, speed, and support.

Finally, themes dictate the appearance of your blog, and while there are dozens of free themes, it's recommended to invest in a premium theme. A poorly designed blog can deter visitors, while a professionally styled one can enhance your brand image.

10.2. Content Creation and SEO

The heart of any blog is its content. Spend time researching and creating high-quality articles. Be consistent in publishing content to show search engines (and your readers) that your site is active.

A crucial aspect of gaining visibility is optimizing for search engines, a practice known as SEO (Search Engine Optimization). Use keywords, meta descriptions, and header tags appropriately throughout your work. Yoast, an SEO plugin for WordPress, will guide you through this process.

Remember to structure your posts with subheadings for easy reading and to include internal links to other articles on your site, as well as external links to authoritative websites for added relevance.

10.3. Monetization Strategies

Once your blog is established and you're producing regular, quality content, it's time to consider monetization. There are several ways to generate passive income from your blog:

1. Affiliate Marketing: This involves promoting other companies' products and earning a commission for every sale made via your affiliate link. Choose products relevant to your niche and genuinely beneficial to your readers.

2. Advertising: Display ads are an easy way to generate income. Google AdSense is a popular choice for bloggers, as it automatically displays ads relevant to your content and audience.

3. Sponsored Content: Companies might pay you to write posts discussing their products or services. Ensure that the product or service aligns with your content and niche.

4. Selling Products or Services: If you wish to, you can sell your own products or services like eBooks, courses, or consulting.

Remember, be patient. Building a profitable blog takes time. The key is to consistently produce high-quality content that offers value to your visitors.

10.4. Building an Email List

A robust email list can increase your earnings significantly. By collecting emails, you can regularly reach out to your audience, promote posts, or endorse products and services. Use call-to-actions (CTAs) to invite readers to subscribe.

10.5. Promotion and Networking

Promoting your blog is a necessary step for gaining traffic and visibility. Use social media, comment on other blogs in your niche, and guest post to establish your online presence.

Networking with other bloggers can expose you to learning opportunities and collaborations which can drive traffic to your blog.

10.6. Continuous Learning and Improvement

The world of blogging technology and SEO practices is ever-evolving. Stay informed of the latest trends, upgrades, and algorithms to keep your blog relevant and appealing.

Remember, running a profitable blog requires hard work, dedication, and patience, but it's a highly rewarding journey that can lead to financial freedom. If you're interested in building a sustainable passive income method, blogging is a fantastic place to start. Embrace the challenges ahead and steadily work toward achieving your blogging and financial goals.

Chapter 11. Striking Gold with Digital Assets: Crypto Investments

The vast lands of digital currencies can often seem like a labyrinth to new investors. This space heralds the future of asset ownership and investment but understanding its many alleyways can seem like quite a task. Let's deconstruct this expansive world and equip you with key information and strategies you need for potential profitable investments.

11.1. Understand the Crypto Space

Although Crypto currencies have been around for more than a decade, the majority of people still find them difficult to understand. At its core, cryptocurrency is a digital or virtual form of currency that utilizes cryptography for security. Unlike traditional currencies issued by central banks, cryptocurrencies are decentralized, working on a technology called blockchain which is a distributed ledger enforced by a network of computers known as nodes.

Bitcoin, created in 2009, was the first cryptocurrency and remains the most well-known and valued one. Since Bitcoin's inception, thousands of alternative cryptocurrencies with various functions and specifications have been created. These are commonly known as altcoins.

11.2. Entering the Crypto Market

Making an entry into this market is fairly simple. All you need is an account with a cryptocurrency exchange and a digital wallet to store your assets. A number of popular exchange platforms exist, like

Binance, Coinbase, Kraken, etc., where buying and selling of digital currencies take place.

Before investing, learning about the following key points can prove helpful.

- **Market Cap:** The total market value of a cryptocurrency. A high market cap signifies a large volume of coins in circulation and a lot of interest from investors.
- **Price:** The current price or value of the cryptocurrency.
- **Volume:** The number of coins that have been traded in the last 24 hours.
- **Circulating Supply:** The estimated number of coins or tokens that are circulating in the market and in the general public's hands.
- **Maximum Supply:** The maximum amount of coins that will ever exist in the lifetime of the cryptocurrency.

11.3. Diversify Your Crypto Portfolio

While Bitcoin by far holds the highest value and is an attractive option, it's crucial to diversify your crypto portfolio. Investing in a range of cryptocurrencies can distribute your risk and increase the possibility of higher returns. Aim to strike a balance between established currencies like Bitcoin and Ethereum, and newer, promising ones.

11.4. Understand the Volatility

The price of cryptocurrencies is highly volatile. Prices can skyrocket in a short period of time, and they can also plummet just as quickly. This volatility can be beneficial for traders looking for quick profits, but it could also lead to significant losses. As such, it's important to only invest money that you can afford to lose and to always maintain a balanced portfolio.

11.5. Long-Term Investing Vs. Short-Term Trading

There are essentially two common strategies when it comes to cryptocurrency investments - long-term (or "Hodling") and short-term (or day trading).

Long-term investment involves buying and holding onto the cryptocurrency for a long period with the intention to sell it at a substantially higher price than what you bought it for.

On the opposite end, short-term trading involves making multiple trades in a day, attempting to profit from the volatility of the crypto market. Both have their own pros and cons and investors should adopt the strategy that best suits their risk tolerance and investment goals.

11.6. Legality and Security

Before investing in cryptocurrency, it's crucial to review the legal status of digital assets in your country, as different nations have different stances toward cryptocurrencies.

One aspect of investing in cryptocurrencies that most investors tend to ignore is their security. Unlike a bank which is insured by the federal government, if your cryptocurrency is stolen, there is no entity that can reimburse you for your loss. Hence, digital asset security should be prioritized. Using hardware wallets can help you store your digital assets securely.

Investing in cryptocurrencies can be a risky venture but it is one that holds the potential for immense rewards. With proper understanding, research, and risk management, you could strike gold within the world of digital assets. Remember, the key to successful investment is education, diversification, and patience.

Incorporating the principles laid out in this guide, you will be well on your way to becoming a seasoned crypto investor, making informed decisions, and potentially amassing great wealth in the crypto world.